HAUNTED
SHREWSBURY

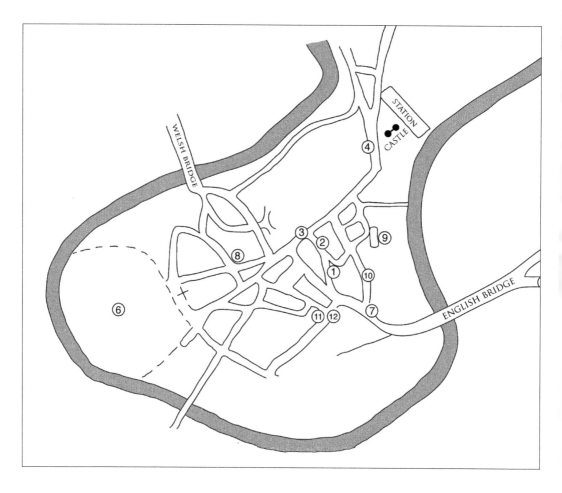

1   FISH STREET

2   BUTCHER ROW

3   PRIDE HILL

4   CASTLE GATES

5   ABBEY FOREGATE

6   THE QUARRY

7   WYLE COP

8   ROWLEY'S MANSION

9   THE PARADE

10   DOGPOLE

11   OLD ST CHAD'S

12   MILK STREET

HAUNTED
SHREWSBURY

MARTIN WOOD

This book is dedicated to my wife, Sue.

First published in 2007 by Tempus Publishing

Reprinted in 2010 by
The History Press
The Mill, Brimscombe Port,
Stroud, Gloucestershire, GL5 2QG
www.thehistorypress.co.uk

British Library Cataloguing in Publication Data.
A catalogue record for this book is available from the British Library.

ISBN 978 0 7524 4303 4

Typesetting and origination by
Tempus Publishing
Printed and bound in England.

CONTENTS

ABOUT THE AUTHOR

Standing at 7ft 2in tall Martin is the world's tallest town crier and has been the official town crier for Shrewsbury and Atcham for the last twenty-one years. During that time he has travelled to Canada, Holland, Belgium and Germany as well as extensively around Great Britain representing Shrewsbury and Atcham in town-crying competitions. He has been the 'Wales and the Marches' champion four times in succession and in the five world championships he has attended he has ranked fifth.

As well as being the town crier, Martin is a toastmaster for weddings and civil functions. He is also a Blue Badge guide and his specialities include 'The Terrible Tudor Tour' for school children (with the blood and gore left in!) and 'The Spooky Shrewsbury Ghost Tour', both of which he conducts on a very regular basis as well as doing illustrated talks to various groups and clubs if they are unable to walk around the town.

He has written and directed a film on the history of Shrewsbury Abbey and in 1984 he had the pleasure of being Edward Woodward's double as the Ghost of Christmas Present and Michael Carter's double as the Ghost of Christmas Future in *A Christmas Carol* filmed in the streets of Shrewsbury. He is also a body double for the character Hagrid from the Harry Potter films.

Martin's main interest is local history and he has appeared on local and national television as well as having programmes on local BBC radio. Martin was also a contestant on Anne Robinson's *The Weakest Link* and finished runner-up to a young lady who was a rowing cox with a university boat crew! Martin's other hobby is woodturning and he travels around the county of Shropshire giving talks and live demonstrations on the subject to groups. Martin is married to Sue and they have two children, Paul and Thomas, both of whom are at university studying music.

Martin in his 'day clothes' as the world's tallest town crier.

FOREWORD

Probably one of the best kept secrets in England is the county of Shropshire. From the rolling hills of the Long Mynd and South Shropshire to the Shropshire plains stretching into Cheshire, the county can boast ancient monuments by the score, medieval towns by the dozen, quaint villages complete with duck ponds, rivers (including the Severn, the longest river in England), canals, one motorway, a couple of small airfields and two big ones, RAF Cosford and RAF Shawbury.

Shropshire can boast many 'firsts': the official birthplace of the Industrial Revolution is Ironbridge, where Thomas Farnolis Pritchard from Shrewsbury suggested a new type of iron to Abraham Darby the 3rd and the first iron bridge was built spanning the Severn, giving the town its now famous name. The first iron-framed building, a flax mill, was built on the outskirts of Shrewsbury and so successful was it that the modern skyscrapers are built still using the same system. Shrewsbury also has many famous 'sons': Charles Darwin, author of *The Origin of Species*, in which he states that we are all related to apes, was born in Shrewsbury and went to school here; Benbow, one of this country's most famous admirals was born here and ran away to sea; Clive of India was mayor and a member of parliament in the 1800s; Percy Thrower became head gardener for the borough, becoming known as the 'Country's Gardener' and was often seen on the children's programme *Blue Peter* nurturing many little green fingers, but the greatest jewel in the town is ... the town itself.

Shrewsbury, the county town of Shropshire, nestles within the horseshoe shape of the river Severn. It was first populated by the Anglo Saxons when the Romans left the area and gave the town its original name, *Pengwern*, meaning 'a hill with alders on it'. When the Normans arrived they renamed it *Scirosabrig*, meaning 'a hill with the alders' (where have we heard that one before?) and used the town to keep the Welsh on the far side of the river which was also the Welsh border. During the Tudor period the town made its fortune in the wool trade with the Drapers. By the seventeenth century the river from Shrewsbury down to the docks at Bristol was reputed to be the second busiest river in Europe with over 700 boats laden with wool, copper, lead and leather being pulled by teams of men called 'luggers' down to the coast and then returning with herbs and spices from far-off countries.

Shrewsbury's medieval streets still carry their original names, evoking the trades that were carried on there: Milk Street where butter, cheese and of course milk was available; Fish Street, mentioned later in the book along with Butcher Row and Barker Street, so called because of the tannery that once stood there and a worker in the tanning business was called Barker. Anyone walking along these streets cannot fail to be aware that they are probably being accompanied by a myriad of people from various times past and all with some wonderful stories to tell, if only we could hear them.

The original half-timbered houses that abound in Shrewsbury still hold their personal memories within the timbers and just occasionally these memories will pop out and walk along routes that were familiar to them many years ago.

Nowadays Shrewsbury is famous for its flowers and festivals, with the West Midlands Agricultural Show in June to the world-famous Shrewsbury Flower Show in August with the street carnival, the cartoon festival, the annual Town Crier's Competition and the street entertainers' festival in between all making the town a 'must visit' place.

Over the past fifteen years I have taken an interest in some of the more spirited populace of Shrewsbury and have researched the reasons why these visitors come back and I hope that these few pages will entice you to visit yourself and experience the peace and tranquillity that Shrewsbury has to offer.

My thanks must go to the various owners of buildings mentioned in this book, especially: Mr Mike Mathews, owner of the Prince Rupert Hotel; Mr Geoff Meredith from Poppy's Tudor Tearooms in Milk Street, Mr Peter Jones, owner of Pete's Clip Joint; and Lads and Dads for allowing us to wander around and photograph various rooms, especially during my tours.

Thanks also to the people of Shrewsbury for recounting their experiences to me and allowing their stories to be published and Mr Nigel Baker, a county archaeologist, for his tales from the cellars of Shrewsbury.

My thanks also to Mr Chris Kennedy, a local paranormal investigator and medium who has helped me immensely in researching the background information of our ghosts and whose name, like that of Nigel's, will crop up from time to time; also to Alan Jones who produced the town map for me.

And finally my most grateful thanks must go to my wife Sue and sons Paul and Thomas for putting up with me as I disappear for a few hours at short notice to research another found spirit.

WHAT ARE THEY?

It is very difficult to explain why ghosts appear and what are they; thanks to some major blockbuster films in the 1980s and '90s a vast majority of people think that a ghost is something that resembles a white sheet with two holes cut out for eyes and which floats 3ft above the ground going 'whoooooo', but this is very far from the truth. Admittedly, some of the sightings have been reported as being like a mist, grey or white in colour, but the majority of the sightings have been of a solid person or persons, or even animals.

Sometimes the spirits can appear on a photograph like a circle of bright light. This is the energy orb that can be picked up by cameras, especially digital ones, but a lot of people don't realise this and think that something has happened to the photographs and delete them. If you see any orbs when your photographs come back, don't bin them!

As to what are they, there have been many books written on this subject and with the new television programmes coming on line and so many ideas put forward that it is quite a minefield so I leave the decision as to why ghosts appear to the individual.

In order to give you a bit of help I try to put ghosts into pigeon holes to make their appearances more explainable: ghosts could be the spirits of people who have been murdered or have lost their life by some human tragedy and are coming back to find the culprit who 'dunnit'; or they could be spirits of people who have committed a crime and are coming back to

Have you ever seen one of these on your photographs? It's not a water mark but an energy orb.

apologise for what they have done; or they are spirits of people who have been buried without a proper religious burial. This third 'pigeon hole' explains why most battle grounds have their fair share of spirits, for example 65,000 men were killed in a three-hour battle at the Battle of Shrewsbury which took place in 1402. The armies did not have the time to bury their dead properly so it is believed that they dug some massive graves and everyone was buried in these. The fourth 'pigeon hole' is that they could be spirits who are just happy being in a particular place or have a happy memory of that area and these are known as memory ghosts

So, having put a few ideas into your mind about why ghosts are about, let's have a wander through some of the streets of Shrewsbury and see what we can see …

ONE

FISH STREET

One of our old town-centre streets, Fish Street is narrow and runs from the upper part of the Wyle Cop to join Butcher Row. The street gets its name from fish that were sold here in the open street market from early in the history of the town. As Shrewsbury was recognised as a very wealthy town, it came with its own mint for a time and had its own weights and measures; tradespeople would come from a wide part of the country. Fishmongers would come from as far away as Hull and Grimsby to the North East and Porthmadog and Barmouth on the Welsh coast, and on a good day the town would host anything up to forty or so fishmongers.

Once the customers had bought their fish, the heads and tails would be cut off and the fish gutted and this would be thrown into the street for the paupers to collect, thus saving the town from paying for a street cleaner, but why? If you did not work, you did not collect any pay and if you had no money then the only food you could get to eat is what you could get from the sweepings off the floor, so the fishmongers would throw all their unwanted bits into the street for the locals to collect, thus helping the town to keep its roads clean.

Dominating the upper part of the street are two giant buildings, the church of St Alkmunds and Bear Steps House. The church of St Alkmunds was originally built in 947 but was taken down and rebuilt in the mid-1700s; interestingly it houses the first iron-framed windows in the world. Ironbridge – the home of the Industrial Revolution and the place where Abraham Darby first smelted iron – is just 15 miles from Shrewsbury and is the site of the first iron bridge, built to span the river Severn. After the bridge was deemed a success the planners then looked around to see what else they could use iron for and the parishioners of St Alkmunds very kindly allowed two iron windows to be placed in the church for 'a trial period'; after 300 years they are still there.

If you look at the church grounds you will note that the majority of the graves are situated around the perimeter of the site as the churchyard was used as the cattle market for the town in the fifteenth and sixteenth centuries.

The second of the buildings, Bear Steps, was built around the late 1300s. It is the standard 'L'-shaped house that was popular around Shrewsbury at this time. It had some sort of shop connected to it on the upper floor, level with the church, and the lower basement part of the house stands in Fish Street itself. This part of the house was originally used as stables or storage rooms but it contains the ghost of a gentleman. Why is he there?

Fish Street; in front of the car is the Bear Steps and to the right is the wall of St Alkmunds.

In 1725 the streets were widened on the orders of the Shrewsbury Corporation to make them safer for pedestrians and the only way to make this possible was to move the wall of the churchyard back. This meant the removal of six graves – the headstones were taken up and placed on the far side of the church but what happened to the remains?

The gentleman ghost that appears in this lower part of Bear Steps is about 5ft 6in in height and wears dark clothing, almost like a suit, and stands at the rear of the shop. Sadly, he makes no effort to speak or make any noise at all but is a very regular visitor to the shop. No murders or serious crimes have been recorded in this place so could he be one of the original 'owners' of this plot of land but was rudely taken up? Sadly, no information is available as to the names of the people who were evicted, so we must assume that he is still looking for his final resting place.

As I write this, the shop is empty but when new owners are found they might find that they have one more 'regular' customer that they bargained for!

On the spire of St Alkmunds can be seen the ghost of a steeplejack who is believed to be one George Archer, although some people refer to him as Robin. It is reported that around 1780 our friend George climbed the spire of St Alkmunds on four separate occasions. On one occasion he climbed to the top armed with a bow and a sheath of arrows which he promptly dispatched over a wide area to prove to folks that his name was Archer. On a second occasion he carried a

Sign of the times, awaiting new owners. The white stone on the left is not a headstone but a marker post.

drum to the top and beat a tattoo to the applause of hundreds of music lovers and twice George climbed the spire to firstly remove and then secondly replace the weathervane from the top. The vane measured 27in from beak to tail and weighed in at around 10lb. These two acts were carried out on the orders of the church and whilst he was up there he entertained the onlookers by dancing a jig. It was said that the reason he managed these feats so well was because he was under the influence of drink on the way up but stone cold sober on the way down! But if that is the case what happened next could be classed as a true tragedy.

George was given the job of replacing the weathervane on top of the new spire when it was built and after his busy day he was resting in the local pub, The Fishes, (now called the Three Fishes, and at the time of writing the only pub in Shrewsbury that has banned mobile phones and juke boxes) when some local gentlemen came in and bet George a gallon of beer that he couldn't climb to the top of the spire and return with the newly fitted weathervane. Naturally George, being a lover of ale, took a while to think about it but as this was his day job he readily agreed and dutifully climbed the spire, removed the weathervane and returned to hand it over to his onlookers who promptly paid up and gave him his gallon of beer. When George had almost finished his seventh pint of the eight, the local gents had a fit of guilt and asked him to return the weathervane, and there would be another drink in it for him if he complied. So up George went again and after he had bolted the vane to the spire, for some reason he stepped

Drunk going up, sober coming down! One of the newly refurbished iron windows can be seen below the tower.

back to admire his handiwork and 180ft later came to a sudden and fatal halt. It was reported in the local broadsheets of the time that George was killed by the fall but that is not the case – it was the landing that did for him.

During the late 1800s the incumbent of St Alkmunds preached to his parishioners that the figure on the spire was not the steeplejack but was in fact the Devil. There is an old Shropshire folklore tale that relates the story of the Devil coming to Shrewsbury to climb the spire and from the top he can look across to the Stiperstones, a range of hills in South Shropshire; on top of the Stiperstones is a rock formation that is known as The Devils Chair and if the Devil spots anyone sitting there then woe betide them! However, although the Sunday morning takings went up for a while this story did not last for very long and George duly returned to claim his place in Shrewsbury's ghost history.

At the lower end of Fish Street stands another church, St Julians. This church was originally dedicated to one of the first lady saints, St Juliana, but was renamed sometime in the 1800s. During the 1980s and 1990s St Julians was converted to a craft market with the owners living in the tower; they still reside there but the building has now reverted to a place of worship.

In the early 1800s people walking along Fish Street could for a while hear screams and shouts coming from behind the church wall, and when the vicar investigated they found that the noise had come from a freshly dug grave. A visitor to the town had been staying at the Lion Hotel and had bought his own chef with him, a gentleman by the name of Taur. One evening the unfortunate chef collapsed when he suffered a choking fit. By the time a doctor arrived the gentleman 'had expired' and the death certificate was duly signed.

Right: *St Julians, last resting place, eventually, of Mr Taur.*

Below: *Granny's flat – shame they have modernised the ground floor, but it's still home.*

For some reason, possibly because there was no known next-of-kin, or that reports of a chef dying in a top hotel in the town would cause embarrassment, the burial took place as soon as the documents had been signed – however, soon after the burial the screams and shouts started, much to the terror of the locals. Eventually the curate of the church traced the screams to the burial plot of the chef. It seems that the visitor was not dead but indeed 'just sleeping' and had been buried alive! Sadly by the time he had been dug up he was properly dead and so was reburied again, possibly the only person to be buried twice in one day in one spot, but for many years screams and moans could still be heard until the craft owners moved in and had the area exorcised. It is said that when Taur was dug up the underneath of the coffin lid had been scraped into grooves and the man's fingers had been worn down.

Another ghost in the vicinity comes via a county archaeologist, Mr Nigel Baker. In the mid-1990s Nigel was part of a team studying over 250 cellars in Shrewsbury. In No. 1 Fish Street, Nigel was talking to the elderly occupants when the lady told him that she had lived in the same house since her early childhood and had been brought up there by her gran. The lady told Nigel that she dared not move any of the furniture or ornaments because if she did then grannie would put them back again. The elderly couple have now passed away but 'grannie' is still there. Upstairs there used to be a hair salon where they got through a lot of trainees as 'grannie' insisted on walking through closed doors and moving things about. The whole building has now been converted to flats but no reports of seeing 'grannie' have been announced yet.

TWO

BUTCHER ROW

As the name suggests, this was the home of the visiting butchers to the town. The street runs from the end of Fish Street and comes out halfway down Pride Hill. Sometimes, if there were too many butchers in the row, the residue would spill out into Pride Hill and this was sometimes known as 'Double Butcher Row'.

The largest of the timber-framed buildings in Butcher Row is the Abbots House. Built in 1457, it was the town house for the Abbots of Lilleshall Abbey. Situated on the Shropshire/Staffordshire border, Lilleshall Abbey was home to over 100 monks in its heyday but the Abbots themselves decided to leave the day-to-day running of the abbey to their deputies and left to reside in other houses. The Abbots, who were interested in making a bob or two, had chosen their site well and had a massive house built in Butcher Row as it was one of the main streets in the town. As well as their own living spaces on the upper levels, they turned the ground-floor rooms into small butcher shops and these were snapped up by the local businessmen.

St Alkmunds was also the site of the town's first cattle market, and on a market day one would be able to find literally hundreds of animals being sold on the site. Once the butchers had set up their stalls in the Abbots House or along the street, they would then go to the market and buy the animals live, lead them back to the stalls and tether them up. When the locals came to buy their meat they could choose the animal they fancied and it would be slaughtered in front of their eyes. Any meat that remained unsold would be hoisted up onto the meat hooks (some of these still remain) and, just like at Fish Street, the innards and any other unwanted bits would be thrown into the street for the poor to pick up.

Many people walking down Butcher Row have the feeling that they are being watched and have reported seeing a 'grey mist with fairy lights' flitting around between the three main windows on the first floor of the Abbots House. As far as I know, no unexplained deaths or murders have occurred in the house so we must only assume that the mist is a mixture of all the animals that have been killed on this site.

Opposite the Abbots House is one of the main town-centre hotels, The Prince Rupert. The hotel is probably the most haunted hotel in Shrewsbury and it contains parts of houses that range from the early 1700s. Named after King Charles I's nephew, Prince Rupert moved to Shrewsbury in 1644 as commander-in-chief of His Majesty's Army and set up his quarters in Jones's Mansion. Jones was an important lawyer in the town and the size of his house was

The three bay windows of the first floor of the Abbots House plays host to a grey mist

testament to his authority. The house is now included within the hotel, and the prince gave his name for it although I doubt if he knew it at the time.

In room 5 could be felt the spirit of a young lady who dates back to the Victorian period. The lady came to Shrewsbury to be married and the day before she was due to walk down the aisle, she discovered that her husband-to-be had run out on her and had in fact married someone else. She, of course, was mortified at this and so upset was she that she took her own life by hanging herself from the beams in the room she was using, room 5.

Her spirit would only visit the room if it was occupied by a young single gentleman staying on his own, and she would remove all the bedclothes! In fact when the present owner of the hotel moved in some fifteen years ago he stayed in that room and on two occasions found his bedding had been moved, once to outside the room and the second time his duvet was discovered in a service lift on the far side of the hotel at 3 a.m. That particular room has now been turned into a small conference room and no more sightings have been reported ... yet.

Some years ago I took a group of young farmers on a ghost tour in early winter and that Christmas at their annual raffle one of the prizes could only be won by a single man – a night in room 5! Later I had the chance to speak to the young winner and he told me that after he had had a meal and a few beers with his mates they went home and he settled down in his room. Just as he was about to fall to sleep someone or something came and knocked on his door. When I asked him if he had seen anything he told me that he had sat up all night with all the lights on and the radio and the television on and by early morning he was ready to go home but he was made to stay for breakfast, but no, he didn't see anything – shame really.

Another three ghosts appear in the basement of the hotel, but they are not connected to each other as far as I can tell. Parts of the hotel date right back to the thirteenth century. One of the

Behind this 1950s Temperance Hotel frontage ...

... lies some of the most wonderful Tudor rooms in the town. This is room 5 where our Victorian bride-to-be called her wedding off in the most dramatic way possible.

The stairs may look level but watch your step! Martha is seen walking here and many guests have felt her presence.

walls that is under the basement floor is believed to be a part of the town's early defences. Very soon after these defences had been built locals started to use them as an outer wall of their own houses and it is this wall that is still under the hotel. During the Norman period a medium-sized pond known as the Dock Pond stood close to where the Bear Steps are now situated. The water from this pond ran off down what is now known as Dogpole and passed behind the houses on Wyle Cop before entering the river Severn. It is the remains of the kitchen that can still be seen.

During the 1980s a medium was staying at the hotel. In a letter to the then manager the medium reported that by going down the spiral staircase into the kitchen a young maid by the name of Martha could be seen and she asked why gunshots were fired. The manager at the time knew that they had no one by that name working in the hotel and they had no spiral staircase either, also if any gunshots had been fired then practically the whole town would have heard it and not just Martha. A short thank-you letter was sent to the medium and everything was forgotten until the present owner, Mr Mike Mathews, took over. He wanted to build a fitness centre and when the builders lifted the old floorboards to lay some foundations they found first a spiral staircase that led down to the old kitchen, and also a skeleton which dated from the mid-1700s, which, surprisingly, was the last known time that a maid by the name of Martha was ever recorded as working there!

The spiral staircase was found under the floorboards and this leads down to the oldest part of the building. It is possible that the steps were actually part of a Norman watchtower before being incorporated in the building.

'Martha' is a very quite lady and often her shadow can be seen standing in the corner of the kitchen, just like a maid would have done, and if you run your hand across the corner about 4ft above the ground you can often feel a cold draught as if she has just moved away. She has also been seen quite recently in the ballroom as an energy orb.

Also in the cellar is the ghost of a small boy who looks as if he dates back to the Tudor period. Thanks to my colleague, Chris, we have found out that his name is 'Thomas' and on many of my tours when we visit the cellar, lots of people spot the young lad standing by the outer retaining wall. On the other side used to be the Dock Pond so did this young lad lose his life in the water?

The owners of the Prince Rupert have recently discovered a doorway that leads into a second room in the basement. This room is in fact under St Mary's Street and was once used by a shop there but recent finds have suggested that this room did in fact belong to the Rupert Hotel, who want to turn it into a wine cellar.

In what will soon be the new wine cellar stands a man who has a fairly angry air about him. He certainly does not like too many people standing in his room and on occasions my tourists have heard him telling them to leave, which they do!

As I am writing this in September 2006, I have just returned from a ghost tour where we visited the cellars just described. As I was explaining about our slightly unfriendly gent, one of the ladies squealed and suddenly caught her necklace of green stones just before it slipped to the

View of the recently opened wine cellar area. The sign on the wall, just visible, is not pointing the way to our 'spirit'!

floor! It seems that the lady's necklace had a screw fitting and as I was talking she felt something, or someone, start to unscrew the fitting! No one was behind her at the time but Chris felt that our friend was about.

Room 7 occupants have reported being woken in the middle of the night by someone sitting on the bottom of the bed and when they look down they can see the outline of someone's posterior in the duvet and on one occasion a gentleman was awoken in the night by someone blowing gently in his ear. Thinking it was his wife he turned over but was disappointed to see she was sleeping soundly. The following night she also was awoken by the same event.

In March 1984, Shrewsbury was turned into a major film set for possibly the most famous ghost story in the world, Charles Dickens's *A Christmas Carol*. The stars of the film, George. C. Scott, Edward Woodward, Susannah York, David Warner and Frank Finlay, all stayed at the Prince Rupert along with the director Clive Donner and the director of photography Tony Imi.

Shortly after the crew had moved into the Rupert, Mr Imi was making his way back to his room after an evening in the restaurant when he saw an old gentleman walking along the passage. The gent was dressed in an old-fashioned nightshirt and was carrying a Wee Willy Winkie-type candle holder. Mr Imi bid him goodnight as he passed him but was slightly disconcerted when the old man totally ignored him and walked through a wall still carrying his candle which Mr Imi then realised that, although lit, was not casting any shadows! After that film members would only make their way to their rooms if someone else was just happening to be going in the same direction.

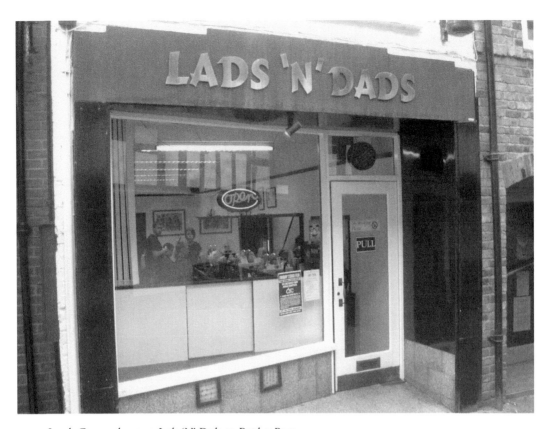

Joseph Coopers shop, now Lads 'N' Dads on Butcher Row.

Close to the junction of Butcher Row with Pride Hill is a gents' hairdressers called Lads and Dads and it is in the rear of this building that the figure of a man, wearing a set of dark clothing but having a brown leather apron around his waist, can be seen. Although it is difficult to place which period he is from we believe that he dates back to the Victorian era and is a 'memory ghost'. In the Tudor times the area was covered by one huge house built by William Owen and his sons but over the years the house was split up and the land taken over by various other owners. The land now occupied by Lads and Dads has been recorded in the past as being a public house and this gent obviously has something to do with the beer trade. In the late 1890s the land was occupied and worked by a beer retailer by the name of Joseph Cooper who expired after suffering from a heart attack lifting or rolling the heavy ale casks. Is the figure that of Joseph still keeping an eye on his goods although they are not there? Or could it be the landlord of the public house still waiting to serve his guests?

THREE

PRIDE HILL

The name Pride Hill should instil terror instantly into any man's heart because it is the realm for women who require a bit of retail therapy – it's the main shopping street in Shrewsbury with many of the well-known high-street stores as well as a lot of small local shops, and it is on the line of this street that the town defences were built by our friends the Normans. And then later in 1275 a much higher stone wall was erected.

Some time after the new walls were built, supposedly to keep the Welsh out, the walls failed to do the job intended and the Welsh, under the leadership of Owen Glyndower, took over the town for a short while until normal order was resumed.

After this the town crier at the time was given permission by the council to shoot with a longbow and arrow any Welshman seen within the walls after curfew on a Sunday (this was normally at 6 p.m.). As far as I can tell, this is still on the statute books and so quite legal.

At the top of Pride Hill stands WH Smith. The original building used to be the house of a family called the Prides who were well known shopkeepers in the 1700s and so the street bears their name, but in 1927 a well-known local firm, Morris's, took over the area and built a huge departmental store where you could buy just about anything you wanted. The store also boasted one of the best ballrooms in the West Midlands and had sumptuous and elegant tea rooms.

Morris's sold their Pride Hill store in July 1970 and it was taken over by John Menzies newsagents before changing hands to become WH Smith. It is here in WH Smith that a young lady appears on the top floor; this floor is almost untouched by modernisation and still retains its original wattle and daub walls and its timber framing (sadly this floor is not accessible to the general public). The young lady in question does not fade away or walk off through a wall – no, she disintegrates!

During the 1300s Shrewsbury had a way of getting rid of unwanted females – they called them witches! Any lady so called was dragged down to the river Severn and crowds would gather by the now demolished St Georges Bridge that once stood at the bottom of Mardol. This was the main entry into the town from the Welsh side and the original bridge had houses and even a pub on it.

A local priest was called upon to bless and so purify the water, the lady was then trussed up like the proverbial Christmas turkey and she was tossed into the water. If the lady sank then she was presumed to be innocent and a proclamation to that effect would be made by the town

WH Smith stands proudly at the top of Pride Hill. The lady with the burning desire to stay, is seen on the top floor.

crier. She would have drowned of course, but she would have been innocent! However, if she floated back to the surface then that would be a sign of her guilt as God would not want such a woman in his purified river. She would then be chased downstream by a few men in their coracles, hoisted out of the river, carried to the highest point of the town walls, and there she would be tied up and burned at the stake. And the highest point of the wall is exactly where WH Smith is now! So, although the flames cannot be seen, the reason for her disintegration is due to her burning, definitely a case of out of the frying pan and into the fire.

No one has actually stayed around to see what happens to her once she's been done to a turn, but there is a probability that at some time in the future a story will emerge of a ghostly caretaker sweeping up certain 'bits' off the floor and putting them out for the binmen!

During the Second World War the building was used as a local meeting place for the soldiers and airmen who trained in the many bases that appeared around Shrewsbury. Here they met with their young ladies and it had a sprung dance floor where Saturday afternoon tea dances and other 'hops' were all the rage. For a long time if you were in the building and it was very quite you could still here the sounds of the big bands playing and hear the heavy boots of the men sliding around on the floor although the floor disappeared many years ago. Recently the Gamezone shop, which occupies a part of the old store, had some work done and when the builders pulled the old floor up a part of the sprung dance floor could still be seen.

Captain Williamson can be seen in the basement of what is now the YMCA shop, below the bicycles. On the right can be seen the site of the Clarendon Hotel, now Burtons.

On the ground floor to the rear of the store stands a young lady dressed in a 1940s-style uniform. She is possibly another of our 'memory ghosts' and was probably here as a tea girl or waitress when the ballroom and tea room were in operation. She has a quiet, calm aura about her and is just happy to stand in one spot.

Some people ask me why there are ghosts in new buildings and I always say that it is not the actual building that could be haunted, but instead it could be the site. One such building stands at the top of the Pride Hill and at the time of writing is home to the YMCA charity shop but it was the original site of the post office in the early part of the 1900s.

During the First World War a certain Captain Williamson of the King's Shropshire Light Infantry had returned from the front for a spot of home leave and was billeted in the Sir John Moore Barracks on the outskirts of the town. The captain knew that he had to return to the front but felt unable to go back and face the horrors of the trenches again, so on 14 July 1916 he wrote a letter of resignation to his commanding officer, went to the post office and mailed his letter, and then went down to the basement of the building, drew his service revolver and committed suicide by shooting himself.

Since the post office moved to a new building just around the corner the old one has been the local electricity-board shop and a fast-food store before being taken over by the YMCA and during these moves a ghost of a soldier has been seen by many of the workers. The ladies who

Left: *Frontage of the Vodafone store. Note that the original timber frames have been replaced by modern timbers.*

Opposite above: *Entrance to retail-therapy heaven, Pride Hill Centre. The perfume shop is to the rear on the right.*

Opposite below: *This view is within the McDonalds store on Pride Hill. The undercrofts in all the houses were much the same as this. You can see the fireplace at the rear, bottom left, but there would have been no large window as this was added at a much later date.*

worked for the electricity board would often describe seeing an army officer complete with 'Sam Brown' belt standing in the storerooms, and indeed, when it was the fast-food store if they ran out of buns or burgers then the whole crew would go downstairs to the refrigerators to pick up the food leaving one member at the top of the stairs with the light on. A friend of mine was once the manager there and when this happened he would dive out of his office, slam the door shut and switch the light off and stand back to wait for the screams!

So don't just look at buildings standing now, delve into the history books and look back and see what used to be there.

Another shop on Pride Hill is now Burtons. This was originally the Clarendon Hotel and in the 1700s it was the venue of a fight between two travellers there. Both of the men were seemingly in the same line of business and so presumably were trying to sign up the same customers. One of the men was stabbed and died at the scene and the other, as was the custom in Shrewsbury at the time, was executed at the rear of the hotel in the stable yard for his crime. The staff working there now have escorted me down to their basement level and as you walk over one particular spot the temperature drops, a sure sign that a presence is there.

Just below Burtons is the Vodaphone mobile phone shop and here at the rear of the shop in the storeroom can be seen a figure of a man. Back in the late 1800s the building was owned by the British & Colonial Meat Co. but by the early 1900s it had been taken over by a single butcher, Mr William Whitall. Could the figure be a memory ghost of one of the long-past butchers or could it be someone from the pub next door, the Greyhound. Looking at the building now, it is a copy of a Tudor house as the timbers used are very smooth, a sure sign of

powered cutting rather than hand sawing and the rooms of the Greyhound would have extended over the butchers. The gentleman in question has been seen standing in the room but he has also been seen sitting on the stairs leading to the back of the shop.

My paranormal investigator Chris, has recently been in and keeps getting the name Robert thrown at him. The man has indicated that he is suffering from chest pains and these could be an indication of a heart attack. So far the only names I have found are William, the butcher, and the landlord of the Greyhound, Richard Fowles.

Another example of previous buildings now built over can be found at the bottom of Pride Hill in what is now a perfume shop in the Pride Hill Centre. The centre houses over fifty shops on three levels and is a haven for shoppers.

Sightings of a young lady have been seen at the rear of the shop and although no name has been found for her she seems to date from around the mid-1700s when the buildings that stood on the site enclosed small shutts or passages that led from the town through the walls down to the river. These passages were dark, sinister places even during the day, and it was only the brave that travelled through them alone, especially as they were also used as part of the red-light district, so was our lady friend just a hapless traveller or was she a lady of the night trying to buy more scent?

Next to McDonalds, halfway up Pride Hill, is a fashion shop that was a shoe shop for many years and was one of the points of interest for the 'Cellar Watch' done by the archaeologists in the 1980s.

There were more than 250 cellars explored around Shrewsbury and the cellars on Pride Hill were of special interest because they were found to be the original undercrofts of the houses built around the mid-1500s. These undercrofts were used as both store rooms, animal stalls and the families' living area and as such all the cooking was done down in these rooms.

Although the manager of the shoe shop at the time steadfastly refused to admit to having a ghost in his store, many of his staff would tell of going down into the basement and would experience something passing them on the stairs, and would also report smelling cooking down there. Was this a family still in residence?

FOUR

CASTLE GATES

The road runs down from the top of Pride Hill down past the railway station and out onto Castle Foregate. At the topmost part, nearest to Pride Hill, it contains some large department stores as well as some smaller individual shops and it is to Woolworths that we now go.

Up to the mid-1950s this area was taken up by the Raven Hotel. This was one of the old coaching inns that had a brick 'skin' put over it to make it look more modern. And it was for a long time one of the major meeting places for the locals. The Raven, or Woolies now, is an integral part of the Darwin Shopping Centre and it is in the basement that a young girl can be seen. No one knows where she comes from or who she is but her description would fit someone from the Victorian period. As the Raven was a major hotel in that era she could have been the victim of a struggle that went wrong after a night out or a young lady of the street. She could even pre-date the hotel to when that area was pleasantly laid-out gardens that swept down to the banks of the Severn. Whoever she is, many visitors to the loading bays see fleeting glimpses of the young lady as she passes through either the hotel or the gardens.

Walking down the hill from Woolworths and looking on your left you can find a small passage that leads to the old police house. It is a dark and very atmospheric place and on the left-hand side is a large building that used to house the town's prison during the Victorian times.

Some years ago a friend of mine, Liz, was working there during the Christmas period when it was a wine shop and at the end of the day she had just finished stock-taking and was making her way back to the front of the store – it used to be Peter Dominics – when she glimpsed a man standing by the window of one of the smaller rooms. Thinking it was one of the other members of staff, she continued downstairs and it was only when she got to the front of the shop that she realised she was the last one down .When the staff all went back to catch the 'intruder' they discovered that there was no one there.

Who was the man and what was he doing there? Easy. The room that the man was in happened to be the room where executions were carried out and he was looking out of the window towards what used to be the old police house. In the house is the ghost of an old policeman who, in his duty, had arrested a man and at the man's trial he was found guilty and subsequently sentenced to be executed.

A short while later it was found that the man had been innocent and the policeman was so overcome with grief that one of his arrests had been wrong that he took his own life. The old

From Tudor, to Victorian, to this, the site of the Raven Hotel. There is even suggestions that Shakespere had a Globe Theatre on this site.

police house used to be a restaurant and at times staff would see a figure suspended in mid-air in the basement as if hanging from a rope. This I believe is the ghost of that policeman. And the figure at the window? Could he be the executed man? But do they appear at the same time? That's not so easy to answer as no one has checked. The manager of the wine store later admitted that on numerous occasions he had the feeling that he was not alone.

For a time there were also reportings of a headless man walking around the police house but I think that was a bit of poetic licence – have you ever heard of a headless man walking? He wouldn't be able to see where he was going!

Moving further on down the street we come to the library that was once Shrewsbury School. Built in the early 1600s from local stone, in its first year it housed around seventy boys but within a year that number had risen to over 200. Apart from a wonderful bronze statue of Charles Darwin outside, visitors can see two statues above the archway. Both these statues depict the uniforms worn by the boys; on the right the boy is holding his hat so that you can see inside it. This means that he is a new boy and his head is empty of learning whilst the lad on the left has his hat held against him so you cannot see inside meaning he is an old boy and his head is full of knowledge.

In its early years the boys were taught in forms, twelve boys to a table, and at the start of each week one young man would be chosen as the form leader. He would be taught the lesson and

Now converted into modern apartments, the hanging cell was the first window at the top of the stairs. The old police house was opposite.

would then have to return to his form and teach the others. At the end of the week they would have an exam and if any boy got a question wrong then it would be the form leader who got the caning, hence the word for a person in charge of a group being foreman.

The building gives off a well-lived-in atmosphere and this author is still seeking people returning books after hours. A good friend of mine, Nigel Baker, who is a county archaeologist, relates a story back in 1978 when he and two other colleagues were excavating and recording an old timber-framed building called Riggs Hall which is connected to the library. The architects and librarians gleefully related ghost stories to the men whenever they could and Nigel admits that being there was slightly scary.

All three men were so busy in the hall that they were actually living there for quite some time and after everyone had gone home and the library had been locked up the creaks and groans from the building could be heard. One evening Nigel was looking into one of their holes whilst the other two were in their kitchen when Nigel heard someone behind him say 'Psst'. He looked around thinking it was a librarian who had returned but to his answer of 'Hullo' there was no response. When he turned back to the excavations he again heard someone say 'Psst' about 3ft from where he was standing. Again he responded with a slightly strained 'Hullo' but there was still no answer. When it occurred for a third time Nigel decided that maybe he would like a cup of coffee and joined the others!

This was not the end of the tale because a couple of months later Nigel ended up working on his own and as a safety precaution he had fitted their kitchen/sleeping quarters with a hasp -and-staple lock to safeguard their tools. Nigel used to go to sleep with the lights and radio on otherwise all he could hear were the creaks of the building and they would keep him awake. However, one night Nigel awoke from his slumber on his camp bed by the sound of the hasp being pushed over the staple and, thinking that he was being burgled, he climbed out of the ground-floor window, rushed around the inner courtyard and let himself in through the main door ... to find that no one was around but the hasp had indeed been pushed over the staple very firmly. In Nigel's own words he finished by saying, 'No one was in the building so that was it – I drove back to the flat I had in Birmingham at the time and got the first decent night's kip in a good few weeks'.

The building next to the library was once the master's house and it has been reported that a figure that sits in a chair by the old fireplace. Maybe it's the ghost of an old master wondering what he could do with one of his pupils, Charles Darwin.

Darwin was born in Shrewsbury in 1809 and was not a brilliant scholar, being more interested in flowers and animals rather than Latin and numbers. Darwin went on to become one of the most famous botanists in the world and wrote his theory of evolution that expounds the theory that all men are related to apes, so it's no wonder that his old school master still returns.

Opposite the library is Castle Gates House. This is one of our lovely timber-framed buildings and its original site was at the top of Dogpole but when the house was sold in the early 1800s it was on the proviso that the new owners moved it so they took the whole house to bits, carted it to its new site and rebuilt it. People walking past the house towards the castle sometimes feel something, whether a child or adult we don't know, pulling or pushing them towards the front door. On a walk one New Year's day with a group of Scottish visitors, one lady was startled to see something grab hold of her coat hem and pull her towards the front door. 'What shall I do?', she asked me. 'Go with it and let's see what happens', was my reply. We watched as she was gently pulled towards the front door and as she stepped onto the mat her coat hem just dropped back, much to her relief! When I knocked on the door the owners admitted that a lot of people ring the bell because they have had the same incidents happen to them!

Why, or rather who, is pulling or pushing them to the house? We have no information about a brutal event happening in the house itself but could this be one of our 'something on the site before' ghosts?

During the Civil War of 1645 the town was a royalist stronghold and it was only when the 'traitor' Captain John Benbow let the parliamentary forces into the town via St Mary's Water Lane on the night of 21 March 1645 did the town fall. The commanding officer of the royalist forces immediately surrendered on the understanding that he be allowed to march his men out of the town. This he did and he and his men went to Ludlow. Sadly a group of Irish soldiers were billeted in Shrewsbury at the time and these poor men were immediately hung without a trial on the day Shrewsbury fell. Apart from those unfortunate Irishmen less than a dozen more men were killed during the entire operation, one of the most peaceful ends to a stronghold's fall in the whole of the Civil War.

Soon after the town had been taken, Captain Benbow realised that he had made a mistake and requested that he be allowed to return to his old unit, now ensconced in Ludlow's castle. In answer to his request, the parliamentary officers took him out and shot him in what was known as the castle's vegetable plot. And the site of the vegetable garden? You've guessed – just about where the castle house is now positioned. So could the unseen pulling power be our errant captain? Or even one of the Irish lads? We may never know.

Front view of Shrewsbury Library. Riggs Hall is to the rear behind the tower and the master's house can just be seen on the left of the main building.

After Captain Benbow was shot he was buried in old St Chad's churchyard. His grave is in the foreground and the remains of Old St Chad's can be seen to the rear.

The old saying, 'If walls could talk' could be used around Shrewsbury Castle. The original Norman fortress, a wooden enclosure atop a man-made hill, has long gone as has the later castle used by Henry IV in 1402 to crush the rebellion led by Henry, or 'Harry' Hotspur, and in its place is a small structure called Laura's Tower that has a commanding view over the town and the surrounding hills.

The great builder Thomas Telford was asked to build a substantial family residence for a prosperous local family by the name of Pulteney in 1787 and he used a lot of the stone from the old castle to build a house, complete with turrets and castellation for the family. Mr William Pulteney was the Member of Parliament for Shrewsbury Borough. The tower was built for Pulteney's wife Laura, and Telford constructed the tower for her complete with seven windows, for a different view of the countryside every day of the week.

Soon after he finished his work Telford became the surveyor for the county and he continued in this post until he died in the year 1834 after a very successful career.

On the site of the castle and before Telford moved in with his builders, there used to stand a house owned by one Mr Jack Blondell. He was an extremely wealthy young man having fingers in most of the business 'pies' in the town. He was a brewer, a draper, owned a string of pack horses and ran a couple of the Severn Trows, large boats used to transport the goods down to Bristol. Jack decided that as he was getting old and nearing his thirty-seventh birthday it would be wise for him to take a wife and father a son to carry on the family name and hey presto the family dynasty would be safe. After much searching through the streets of Shrewsbury he found

Opposite: *One of our finest houses at the entrance to Shrewsbury Castle. This house originally stood at the top of Dogpole but was moved timber by timber a distance of around half a mile and not a Pickfords van in sight! The Irish men were hung to the left of the building and the person with the pulling power did not have to use the Land Rover!*

Right: *The climb to Laura's Tower is worth it for the stunning views towards South Shropshire, as long as it's not raining!*

the love of his life, proposed to the young lady, was accepted, and all the church bells in the town rang and the townsfolk toasted their good health and everyone lived happily ever after ... for about sixteen months. Then, 'Oh woe is me, my wife has left me, what shall I do? I know, I'll get married again', which he did to Mrs Blondell No. 2. Again the bells rang and the townsfolk toasted the new bride, and all was well for a while until once again, 'Oh woe is me, my wife has gone, what shall I do?' Answer – get married again. So along came Mrs Blondell No. 3 and then sometime later Mrs Blondell No. 4 and then Mrs Blondell No. 5, and by the time he got to No. 6 the townsfolk were a bit tired of toasting his new brides. Mrs Blondell No. 6 was the only wife to remain in Shrewsbury. She was the sister of Mrs Blondell No. 5 and wanted to know where her sister and the others had gone as people were starting to talk.

One fine day Mr Blondell had to go into Wales on business and on bidding his wife a fond farewell drove his carriage through the town and across the St George's Bridge into Frankwell and on into Wales. On his return some two or three weeks later, he was met at the door of his house not by his wife but by the sherriff of Shropshire who promptly charged him with murder and locked him in the prison. While Jack was away Mrs Blondell No. 6 had been wandering around the huge house and had gone into Jack's private rooms. There she had opened a cupboard, and found five complete sets of fingers laid out.

At his court case it transpired that after Jack had got fed up with his wife he passed her on to his servants and when they had got fed up with the young lady then she was killed and her body thrown over the garden wall, straight into the river, to be taken downstream towards Bristol, but

Shrewsbury Castle is now host to the Shropshire Regimental Museum. Jack appears outside the ground-floor door directly in front of the camera.

before the body was launched on their last journey Jack would chop off the fingers and that is what his final wife found. At his trial Jack gained the nickname 'Bloody Jack'. He was found guilty and was hanged on the gibbet at Old Heath, on the outskirts of the town, but his ghost still walks the castle grounds to this day.

Sometimes he is seen being followed by a group of women who appear to be crying but most often he is seen on his own. His ghost appears by a door on the ground-floor level and he walks across the castle's frontage and lawn before disappearing, always at one particular spot. This is now known to be where the Normans had built their chapel and Jack will always disappear where the outer wall of the chapel once stood.

Inside the castle which is now the Regimental Museum a pair of boots can be heard walking across the balcony. This is most disconcerting as the balcony was removed nearly thirty years ago but the boots still continue walking.

Some twenty years ago the castle was a target for the IRA and almost £4 million-worth of damage was done but as the workmen were arriving for another day's work they would find that their tools had gone missing and were turning up in all sorts of places. Is this Jack's work or had the boots got some arms as well? It must be noted that a group of volunteers spent months re-ribboning thousands of medals that had been donated to the museum and had been damaged by the fire. We also had a lock of Napoleon's hair replaced. Thank you Mrs Napoleon.

One of the finest stations in the land. Built in the early 1800s, it was subsequently enlarged by adding a new lower ground floor by excavating the basement out – clever stuff.

Below the castle stands Shrewsbury's railway station. Built in the early 1800s, it is arguably one of the nicest station buildings in the country. It quickly became a major link between London and North Wales, and Cornwall and the North East. The first line was to Chester and on the opening day of the line the good folk of Chester locked the ticket seller up so that no one could buy tickets to Shrewsbury.

During the heavy winter of 1888 a local coal merchant and MP, Mr Thomas Thomas, arrived at the station and was driven in his carriage up onto platform three to await the London train. Sadly for Mr Thomas, just as he arrived on the platform the weight of all the snow on the ornate glass roof caused it to collapse, and Mr Thomas Thomas was no more. Platform three is normally used for the Chester trains now but many travellers on the other platforms can be seen to wave and shout to a dark-suited figure standing on his own by the ornate gates as they try to tell him that not many trains use that side anymore. But he continues to wait for the train to London, as does everyone else!

Another tragedy occurred at the station in 1907. When the brakes of a post-office platform trolley failed and the trolley rolled onto the line, two post-office workers jumped onto the tracks to try and pull the trolley free, but both were killed by a passing train. Once again, people walking past that point can suddenly feel a chill.

Opposite the station is the Gala Bingo hall but up until the 1970s it was the old Granada Theatre. Many famous acts have appeared here in the past including Laurel and Hardy, Mrs

The ornate entrance to platform 3, Mr Thomas appears to the left of the gates.

During its heyday as a theatre even the Beatles played here. Now it's housey, housey all week. The pizza bar is the last building on the right.

Mills, Norman Vaughan and even the Beatles! As well as the live theatre it was also a cinema and Saturdays would see the local kids attempting to get in without paying. One young lady who did succeed continued to do so on a regular basis as someone who lost her life in one of the upper circle boxes. Reports of this lady were quite common during the Granada days but it seems that she may not like bingo as she has not been seen for a long time, or is it that the staff don't like to admit she's there?

Next to the bingo hall is a pizza shop which Chris has visited recently, and it is in here that the ghost of a male usher can be found, and sometimes he can be heard, asking people to, 'Move on, please'. It seems that this chap likes to wander into the ladies' toilet which must be a bit disconcerting!

FIVE

CASTLE FOREGATE

Continuing to walk out of the town and into the suburbs along Castle Foregate you pass the large imposing buildings belonging to Morris's where they produce their motor lubricants. Originaly this was the site of the Corbet Perserverance Ironworks built in 1873, and it was a leading employer in the town until it was virtually destroyed by fire in the November of 1905. Morris's bought the old factory in 1929, moved all their oil production there from various parts of the town, and the name 'Golden Film' lubricants oiled the engines of motors across the world.

The yard at the rear of their factory was once the terminus basin for the Shropshire Union Canal before the canal was taken up and the railways were laid, enabling more supplies to be bought in and sent out across the country, and it is here at the top of the steps leading up to one of the buildings that the the ghost of an old worker can be seen. He wears a brown work coat and a bowler hat that suggests that he could be some sort of foreman dating from the early 1900s coming back to check on his lads and making sure that they don't slacken! He has a very genial air about him so he must have been a popular man in his time.

A second fire occurred on the site in 1954 and although no official reports of any losses were announced, local men have told of seeing our 'foreman' walking around – could our bowler-hatted friend have been checking that all his men were safe?

The clock tower of Morris's Lubricants stands above the old Corbet Perserverance Ironworks.

SIX

ST MICHAEL'S STREET

Another railway-related haunting occurs on the premises of Salop Music Centre on St Michael's Street. On 17 October 1917, the Irish Night Mail from Crewe approached the Crewe bank curve just outside Shrewsbury station and witnesses speak of seeing the footplate crew arguing just before the train – '... travelling at the breakneck speed of 60 miles per hour' – left the track; in the ensuing crash more than twenty-seven people were killed. Where Salop Music Centre now stands used to be a funeral parlour, and the bodies from the crash were taken there. Customers and staff in the sheet-music department often have the feeling that they are being followed but when they look around there is no one there. Staff at the centre have also reported coming in to work only to find music scattered around on the floor or books moved to different shelves. Three men from Shrewsbury who were working on the Night Mail were amongst those killed.

Just along the road from the music centre is the main fire station for Shrewsbury. During the eleventh century there used to be a small monastery on this site and even now on a quiet day or evening the figure of a monk can be seen slowly making his way across the drill yard. Is he going for some fire drill or is he in fact making his way to the church for compline? Many a new recruit has had practical jokes played on them by their older firemen colleagues suddenly emerging with a sheet over their uniforms, but when asked most of the lads will admit to being a little bit spooked out by the general feeling of the area.

One place that you would possibly expect to see plenty of ghosts is at the site of the gallows but in fact there are very few ghosts seen. The reason for this is that usually a condemned person is normally escorted to the gallows by a priest or had one spend the night before his execution with him in his cell.

Many of the accounts of executions finish with the words, 'The felon had made his peace with his maker before he was launched into eternity', thus he was a happy and contented man, or as happy and contented as he could be knowing that he was about to be executed at first light, and so had no need to re-visit the crime scene.

Above: *The driver and fireman of the Night Mail was seen by the signalman arguing whilst the train was travelling at 60mph. Moments later it crashed just beyond the curve killing twenty-seven people including both the footplate men.*

Left: *Site of the gallows at the top of Pride Hill. The cross was presented by the boys of Shrewsbury School.*

SEVEN

OLD HEATH

Going about 2½ miles out of town along St Michael's Street, travellers will pass through a housing area called Ditherington, up Heath Gates Bank, and then come to a major traffic island. This is the spot where the gibbet used to be and the area is still known as Old Heath.

The youngest person to be executed on this spot was a seventeen-year-old girl whose crime was to steal a lace handkerchief. Her ghost can still be seen but very rarely. Heath Gates Bank was once called Hangman's Hill and it was a favourite spot to stand and watch the hangings and maybe buy a flagon of ale and a side of beef and have a party! The more the condemned man, or woman, struggled or screamed their innocence, the better the atmosphere and the crowd was normally on the side of the condemned, but if they went quietly then it wasn't a good hanging.

Believe it or not this was once a pleasant walk up to the gallows, now it's a major road into the town. You could be killed crossing this bit – that would have saved time!

EIGHT

DITHERINGTON

One possible reason why Ditherington got its name is that where the bus depot is now based there used to be a small prison and it was here that prisoners spent their last night before walking up to Old Heath. The local slang for shaking was to 'dither' as was the term to walk slowly, so the frightened felons would dither like mad as they went to their fate, and the area was known as Dithering Town before it was shortened to Ditherington.

Having said all that, in the early seventeenth century it was normal in Shrewsbury for criminals to be hung close to the site of the crime. Most of the executions were carried out as soon as the attacker was caught, leading to a few innocent people facing a 'long drop' from the branches of a nearby tree, or in the case of one murder in 1694 the guilty man was suspended out of a window of a pub that was built in the centre of the English, or Stone, Bridge and his body hung there for seven days before he was cut down and his body left to float off downstream. Again, as in a lot of places in Shrewsbury, people can sense a cold spot at the site of where the pub stood and this is a theory that runs throughout the town. As a lot of fights occurred in public houses then it is no wonder that there are a few extra customers still hanging around.

During the early 1800s it was a custom in Shrewsbury for locals to apply to visit the body of an executed prisoner after it was cut down as the laying of hands on the body would help to cure 'wens'. This was a local name for arthritis but if the cure was successful or not we don't really know. A bit more gruesome than taking tablets anyhow.

The condemned person would spend their last night in a prison here before walking to the gallows. During the Second World War the Spitfire wings were fabricated here before being shipped out to Castle Donnington.

NINE

ABBEY FOREGATE

This street gets its name from the huge abbey church that dominates the area nearest to the town. Built by Roger de Montgomery who was a nephew to William the Conqueror, the abbey was erected to appease the locals' anger after Roger had dozens of houses destroyed to clear the area around his castle.

Before the Normans arrived a small wooden church stood on the site and when Roger arrived he laid his gauntlets at the altar and decreed that, 'Here will stand the finest Abbey in the land'.

During the building of the abbey, Roger was bitten by the religious bug and entered the order as a lay monk. He only just made it because less than three months later he was dead! Roger was buried inside the abbey as a mark of respect but when Henry VIII came along to dissolve the monasteries, Roger's effigy was unceremoniously chucked out for a couple of hundred years until he was rediscovered and put back in his rightful place.

Sadly a lot of the old inns have disappeared from Abbey Foregate in the name of progress, but fortunately one is still there. The Old Dun Cow is almost untouched by modernisation and has a wonderful welcome for all travellers. However, it has two spirits – and not the liquid type either – that wander around the pub.

One is the figure of a monk supposedly from the nearby abbey church. If this particular monk doesn't like you then he has the tendency to give your table a kick, spilling your beer on the floor before hitching his cassock up and walking off to find more mischief.

The second ghost is that of a seventeenth-century Dutch army officer. During this period Holland was at war with Spain and it was a regular occurrence for Dutch officers to come over to this country to recruit men for the Dutch/Spanish War. This one particular day an officer had arrived in Shrewsbury from the Netherlands and as he reigned in his horse outside the Dun Cow he ordered a local man to carry his bags inside for him. Now, one thing about Shrewsbury folk, they don't like taking orders from strangers and this lad was no exception so he rightly refused the officer's command, at which point the Dutchman drew his sword and promptly killed the local man.

Witnesses to this act of murder were rightly upset and the Dutchman was immediately caught, bound and brought before a court of locals. In his defence the Dutch officer was heard to say, 'Well I only killed one Englishman'. This so incensed the locals that they sentenced him to be hung immediately and so he ended his life suspended from a tree in Abbey Foregate.

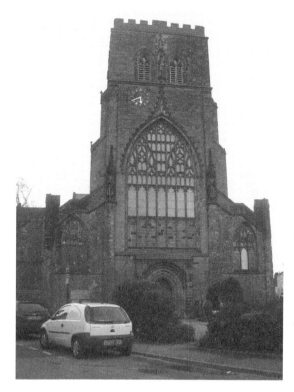

Left: *The immense tower of the Abbey dominates all around. Not only famous for its connections with Roger and the Normans, it is also the home to the fictional super-sleuthing monk, Brother Cadfael.*

Below: *A warm welcome awaits travellers from the staff, and the monk, of the Dun Cow. The Dutchman was hung from the branches of a tree outside the pub, better that than saying he was hung from a bus shelter!*

Abbey Foregate is a mix of house styles from just about every period. The entrance to Cold Bath Court is to the left of this wonderful Tudor house.

Some years ago a young couple who were on their honeymoon were staying at the Dun Cow when the young man needed to go to the gents to wash his hands. As he stood there in the gents he spotted this Dutchman and his first thought was that there was going to be a fancy-dress party. It was only when our Dutchman walked through a wall that the lad took off, grabbed his bride and three hours later phoned from a hotel in Leeds asking for their suitcases to be forwarded on to them!

Slightly further along the Abbey Foregate is a short passage originally known as Cold Bath Court but now included in a private dwelling where a group of dark-robed monks are sometimes seen to be walking down the passage on their way to the Rea Brook for their weekly bath. The water was so cold they could catch their death … so that's why they are there!

TEN

MEMORIES

There are those spirits that are known as 'memory spirits', a particular ghost that appears at a spot where it has, or had, special memories during its lifetime. Many examples of these types of spirits are usually found around family homes.

One example is from a lady in Nesscliffe, 6 miles from Shrewsbury, who was in her kitchen one morning when she happened to look down her garden, and saw her father looking and smiling up at her. Twenty minutes later she received a telephone call from her mother in Australia telling her that her father had just had a heart attack and had passed away. The lady in Nesscliffe was certain that her father had come back to see her once more and maybe to let her know that everything was alright.

Another example of this type of memory ghost used to appear in Telephone House, a large 1960s concrete and glass building that used to stand on Smithfield Road in the town. This particular ghost is a Norman soldier who used to appear on the fifth floor of the building. Now we know for certain, because it is well documented, that the Normans never had telephones, so what was he doing there? It can't have been for not paying his phone bill, that's for sure! Part of the original town walls ran along that stretch of the road because on the other side of the road was the river, and our Norman friend is in fact on sentry duty on his part of the wall, making sure that the Welsh didn't come calling.

It is just a shame that someone saw fit to erect this building on top of him. The building itself is no longer there and as no one has seen a ghost standing in mid-air we must wait for a new building to be erected and who knows, he may hopefully return to resume his sentry duty.

On London Road is a house belonging to some friends of mine and they used to have a Victorian butter dish hanging on the wall. This was a very ornate dish and if you walked past it during mealtime you could smell butter on it but not at any other time.

In Bicton, a small village just out of town, a lady lived in a bungalow next to the church and on numerous occasions she would come home to find that all her doors had been locked from the inside and on one occasion she came home to find a child's Victorian coat-hanger lying on the bed. Despite contacting the police no one came forward to claim the hanger so she held on to it for quite a while, until it disappeared, never to be seen again. It transpired that the bungalow had been built on an old, disused part of the churchyard that had been a children's plot, so maybe a few occupants had been having some childish fun.

Pleasantly calm view of Smithfield Road. Telephone House stood on the left, and to the right of the line of trees is the river Severn.

Sadly some of the information on Shrewsbury ghosts are a bit on the sketchy side. One of the main reasons for this is that most people are a bit hesitant in admitting they have seen a ghost due to the possible ridicule that they may face. On my tours of Shrewsbury I always begin by asking how many people believe in ghosts and quite a few hands are raised but when I ask how many people have seen a ghost the majority of hands stay down. However, during the walk people come up to me and say, ' I don't know if it's a ghost but ...' and then out comes a tale that if you can corroborate then you have another possible convert.

A lot of children have often talked about fairies at the bottom of the garden. Are these just figments of their imagination or are they real ghosts? Perhaps children are very good at seeing things that we adults can't. How many times have you told your child that there's no such things as fairies, dragons, giants, ghosts?

A child has an open mind but as parents and other adults continue to tell them, 'There's no such thing as ...' then they begin to build mental walls and eventually these walls become impregnable and so we lose someone's information, hence some of the sightings becomes sketchy.

Okay, soapbox bit over, let's get back to our friendly ghostly visitors.

ELEVEN

THE QUARRY

During the Second World War Shrewsbury was surrounded by Royal Air Force Operational Training Units. These units taught the young pilots to fly before they were transferred to the frontline squadrons but, unfortunately, they tended to use out of date and much repaired aircraft and so they had a habit of not being too reliable.

One of the antics the pilots took part in was the Shrewsbury challenge: this involved the pilots flying low along the river as it passes through the town's public gardens and the quarry, going under the Kingsland Toll bridge and then pulling up into a tight curving climb before they crashed into the chimney stack of a nearby brewery. Generally, all the pilots managed this feat but one pilot failed to make the passage under the bridge and is still down there in his aircraft, it being deemed to dangerous to lift as the water is too deep in that area,

A ghostly figure of a man has been seen standing on the banks of the river beside a statue of Hercules. On a recent walk with a group of locals, Chris was joined by some of the lads from the tour and along with his electronic gizmos found the man and came up with the name 'William'. Could the ghost be that of the pilot? Or is it another of our 'memory spirits'? Either way, the lads on the tour decided to visit a nearby hostelry pretty smartly.

The quarry itself is a large 8-acre site that sits on the bend of the river Severn and in August of each year becomes home to the world-famous flower show. Over 100,000 visitors flock to the show for a feast of flowers and military music and the whole area is a hive of beauty and activity.

The quarry was where a lot of the stone was taken for buildings in Shrewsbury and the hole that was left became 'The Dingle'. This was completely planted out by the late Percy Thrower who was head gardener for the Borough and also the *Blue Peter* garden adviser for many years.

Hercules stands alongside the river Severn. The Kingsland bridge can just be seen through the trees to his left.

TWELVE

IT'S A PERSONAL THING

On my many ghost tours around the town one question is always asked of me, 'Have you ever seen a ghost?' and my reply is always the same, 'Yes'

After marrying my wife Sue, we moved into a 1950s-built semi-detached house on the outskirts of town and the house had an extension that we used as a workshop. It was not long before we realised that we were not the only residents of the property as tools would move around and sometimes if we were working in there on our own we could sense that the other had come in but when we turned around no one was there. When our first son, Paul, was born we turned the workshop into a playroom for him and from the kitchen we could hear Paul talking to someone. When he came in he would tell us that he had been playing with his 'friend' but when our second son, Thomas, was born, Paul's friend disappeared.

If we were in the kitchen/dinning room of the house we could see a set of whisks that used to hang from a rack swing backwards and forwards; if you told 'Fred' to stop then the swinging would cease and the back door open then close, just as if 'Fred' had gone off in a huff. After a bit of detective work we discovered that the ground our housing estate was built on was a campsite for Henry Percy's followers. Percy was opposing King Henry IV at the Battle of Shrewsbury in 1403. Result? The King won and Percy's head was put on display at the top of Pride Hill for all to see.

THIRTEEN

OUT IN THE COUNTRYSIDE PART 1

The reportings of ghosts on the county roads around Shrewsbury stretch back for many centuries and the following are just a few of those spectral pedestrians.

On the Ellesmere Road leading out of the town towards the North are the ghosts of two children who can be heard playing in the fields alongside the road known locally as Winney Hill, a great place in the winter to hone your tobogganing skills.

During the Second World War Shrewsbury got off very lightly with war damage even though it was used as a staging post for all the supplies of arms, ammunition and men coming from the docks at Liverpool and North Wales, and the town was even used as a marker for the German bombers on their way to the docks at Liverpool.

On one such bombing run the pilot of the bomber spotted the moon's reflection on what he thought was the docks and subsequently dropped his load of bombs. In fact, the reflection he saw was the moon reflecting off the glass of some large greenhouses on the Ellesmere Road. The bombs landed close to a house where two children from the Midlands had been billeted and in the ensuing blast both of the children and the owner of the house were killed. Pedestrians walking along can still hear them playing.

Also on that stretch of road is the ghost of a motorcyclist. At one point the road passes through a tunnel of trees and it is here that the locals out walking their dogs can hear the sound of a motorbike struggling up the hill, but as the bike passes you and the sound recedes you realise that you cannot see the bike or rider. Who is he or where does he come from?

Another roadside ghost appears on the Baschurch road. Returning from a night out with friends of my parents, we were travelling along the road at around 2 a.m. when, in my headlights, I picked up the sight of an old lady walking along the road laden down with two suitcases. Pulling up in front of the lady, my mother jumped out and asked the lady if she wanted a lift somewhere but the lady had disappeared, suitcases and all. Although we spent some while searching the fields on both sides of the road, she had vanished into thin air. It transpired that in the 1940s a lady was walking to Baschurch, about 10 miles from Shrewsbury, to spend some time with her pregnant daughter when she was knocked down and killed on that road. The lady still continues her never-ending walk to see her daughter.

One roadside ghost that I have heard of has only been seen once to my knowledge. I was giving a talk to a ladies group in the small village of Cressage, between Shrewsbury and

Remember a thing called snow? Well, when we get it this place is busier than the M6! But on a quiet day the voices of children playing can be heard.

Ellesmere Road leading out of Shrewsbury. Sometimes a motorbike is heard growling up the hill, but it is never seen,

Never pick up strangers. An old lady has walked this route since the 1940s on her way to Baschurch, some eight miles on … she never arrives.

Bridgnorth. At the end of the talk a lady approached me and told me that a while ago she was with her husband walking their dogs when a hearse passed them on its way to Shrewsbury. There were no other cars with the hearse but both the husband and wife clearly saw a young girl of about five or six kneeling beside the coffin with her arms draped across it. The hackles of one of the dogs rose and it began to growl, but as the hearse and its occupants moved away the dog calmed down. Was this a young girl, lost in infancy, escorting her mother to her final resting place?

Further out of Shrewsbury near to the village of Shawbury can be found a slightly more mobile ghost that appears on the road to Moreton Corbett. Motorists have reported travelling down the road when they run into a greyish mist that seems to cling to the car for about 500 yards before dissipating. Could it be the spirits of the Corbetts who began to build a house in that area but never finished it?

When the house was begun, a local man by the name of Holmyard quarrelled with the Corbetts and laid a curse on the house, saying that no Corbett would live there. The house was never finished so could this mist be the Corbetts looking for their residence or could it be Mr Holmyard making sure the travellers are not of the Corbett family.

At a spot on the main road between Much Wenlock and Bridgnorth there is the ghost of a lady known as the 'Mary Way' ghost. This lady is a little frightening as she appears headless and

The very desirable residence of the Corbet family at Moreton Corbet just needs a few finishing touches, that's all.

The island at Weeping Cross, no longer a resting place for the departed, just a site for traffic signs.

dressed in white. It transpires that the lady was murdered along this lonely stretch of road and her ghost appears both at the spot where she was murdered and also at her burial place. She is known as the Mary Way ghost after a religious procession that used to pass along this way during the early seventeenth century.

Nearer home at Weeping Cross Island, on the old Shrewsbury by-pass, is a group of mourners who have been visiting the same spot for over 400 years. From the end of Abbey Foregate the road turns into Sutton Road and there you will find the parish church of St Giles. The church has been there from the Norman times and it was a leper church so families bringing their kin to be buried could only fetch them as far as Weeping Cross and the monks would collect the bodies and bear them to the church themselves.

Between the traffic island and the church is Springfield School and many times staff and pupils have seen the ghost of a lady walk through the school. Is she on her way to meet with a funeral group, or just a lady on a regular walk? Another one for Chris to look into!

Now that we have had a little trip out into the country let's pop back into town and look at some more indoor ghosts – we will nip back into the wilds later.

FOURTEEN

WYLE COP

The name Wyle derives from the Welsh word *Hylfa*, meaning hill, and the Wyle Cop is the main route into the town from the Abbey Foregate. The English Bridge spanning the Severn to the gradient part of the hill is known as Under the Wyle and on the left-hand side is an antiques centre. At the rear of the centre is a building that dates back to the eleventh century and was once used as a mortuary. There are certain parts of the old building in which customers or staff experience 'sensations' Are these residual spirits of people long gone? I think so.

The Wyle Cop is the hill itself but it is known locally as just the 'Cop' and it is dominated at the top by the only original coaching inn left in the town, the Lion Hotel

The hotel was built in the late 1700s and boasted an Adams-style ballroom. Some of its more famous guests included Charles Dickens and Jenny Lind. Even William IV stayed here, mind you he was only the Prince William then but it helped to give the hotel a good name in those days! Many hundreds of thousands of guests have passed through this wonderful hotel as they journey across our country but there are some of the guests who still reside there. As previously mentioned, the hotel includes an Adams-style ballroom and at the time of writing the hotel has recently 'peeled away' years of paintwork to find the original décor so the ballroom is now back to its original state. Leading from the ballroom is a curved staircase that takes guests back to the reception area and at the foot of the stairs stands a lady dressed in a powder-blue dress. She appears to be waiting for someone but then turns and leaves, walking through the outer door. The most upsetting thing about this lady is that the door is no longer there but has been replaced by a wall. From the outside you can still see the lintel. Was she a casualty from a coaching accident?

When coaching was in its heyday around the mid-1830s, one of the most famous coaches to run from London to Shrewsbury was 'The Wonder'. This was driven by a local celebrity by the name of Sam Haywood. Sam's main boast was that he could do the journey from the capital to Shrewsbury in sixteen hours and would time his arrival at the Lion almost to the second. People would stand at the top of the Cop and watch in awe as he drove his coach and four up the hill, execute a complete circle before driving under the arch and deposit his passengers in the hotel. Sam drove this coach for over twenty years and in all that time was never more than ten minutes late, and never hit the wall once although there was only 1in clearance on each side! Did another coachman try to emulate Sam, without success, and in doing so catch the unfortunate lady? Sadly we will never know for sure.

The Lion Hotel dominates the top of the Wyle Cop. To its left is the house that Henry stayed in on his way to Bosworth.

Some short while ago the young night porter on duty had occasion to go to a customer's car late at night and on the way back into the hotel he spotted the lady standing in her usual place at the foot of the stairs. So frightened was he that he walked straight up to the reception desk, wrote out a letter of resignation and left immediately. To our knowledge the young man has never been back to the hotel but our lady in blue was not worried about the event and is still there.

Another haunting in the hotel occurs in a room situated above the stairs. At some time in the past a murder or other terrible crime has been committed in the room. The hotel owners are very quiet about what happened and some years ago the staff refused to enter on their own as they could sense an atmosphere, almost of hatred, in the room. So terrible was this atmosphere that in the end the room was bricked up but sounds of groans and moans could be heard and for a while a lighted candle could sometimes be seen in the window – how did it get there?

Still in the Lion Hotel, a story emerges of a time some eighteen years ago when the hotel was playing host to a world-famous pianist. The pianist sent his own personal tuner to make sure that the piano was to his satisfaction and once this had been done then all the staff were on pain of death if they even breathed on the piano, let alone touch it! So imagine the duty manager's anger when she was woken in the middle of the night by someone tinkling on the ivories! She rushed out of her room across the balcony and was leaning over to berate the staff when she

The lady in the powder-blue dress keeps warm by the radiator at the bottom of the stairs then walks out to the left of the bench.

realised that the piano lid was still shut, but whoever was there had the ability to move through wood and could play wonderfully well.

On the opposite side of the Wyle Cop to the Lion and slightly downhill stands the old Nags Head pub. The pub dates back to the Tudor period but some of the building has now fallen into disrepair so only the frontage is used.

On the top floor of the pub is a room with a mysterious secret. Inside the room is a cupboard and on the back wall of the cupboard is a painting, supposedly of a prophet. The story goes that if anyone looks on the painting then they will develop madness, something that has happened at least three times to our knowledge. The first occurrence happened when a maid who worked at the Lion Hotel was in the room helping out. She moved the cupboard to clean behind it and that same evening threw herself out of the window to land under the wheels of a passing stagecoach, and was killed outright.

The second death happened not long after when a coachman who had just secured a job with a landed gent had dropped his charge off at the Lion and then moved into his room in the Nags Head. The following morning he was found suspended from the rafters in the room. The third death occurred during the First World War when an army officer was staying in the room. He shot himself with his service revolver. After this event the room was locked and bricked up until the 1980s when it was reopened. During the 1960s and 1970s the landlord of the pub

Above: *View of the ballroom in the Lion Hotel with the balcony in front and the Adams fireplace just in shot on the right.*

Left: *The three unfortunate guests all stayed in the topmost room which have 'Yorkshire' sash windows; they slide across rather than up and down*

Opposite above: *Faces of soldiers killed at Bosworth appear at the windows of this popular pub in Barracks Passage.*

Opposite below: *All the buildings on the left were once the site of Mr Jones's mansion. The car is just on the English Bridge.*

Dozens of the little blighters! Sheep or men we do not know, but there are a lot of them.

Pete the hair stylist 'in conversation' with the orbs, 'Short back and sides, sir?'.

experienced a very noisy ghost. This particular spirit would turn the juke box on at differing times through the night and if the landlord shouted at the ghost then he, or she, would just turn the volume up! Strangely this only occurred during the summer months. The landlord had no problems during the winter time so I wonder if a pub in Spain has a ghost that appears to turn the music up only in the winter?

Virtually opposite the Nags Head pub is Barracks Passage and this is another site of a memory ghost. In 1461 Henry, Earl of Richmond was on his way to Bosworth in the hope of defeating King Richard and rightfully gaining the crown of England. Henry had stopped in Shrewsbury for a few days to rally support and to recruit more men for his army and he stayed in what is now called Henry Tudor House, just below the Lion Hotel.

His officers were billeted in the Lion and Tap public house in Barracks Passage and because of the warm welcome from the folks of Shrewsbury a lot of the officers killed at the Battle of Bosworth return to spend some time in the place they were happy.

Result of the battle? Richard was killed, Henry was crowned on the battlefield and, as he was the last of the House of Lancaster, he went and married Elizabeth of York and so the War of the Roses was at an end – hurrah!

At the bottom of the hill on the approach to the bridge is Pete's Clip Joint and in the cellar of the building is the largest collection of energy orbs that I have seen. Pete and his wife came on one of my ghost tours a short while ago and took a photograph in the Prince Rupert. The photograph showed an energy orb which they were thrilled about. A few days later Pete thought he would take some shots of his cellar and bingo – photo after photo kept showing these orbs, some of which are coloured, but why so many?

In 1638 the area was owned by one man, Thomas Jones. Mr Jones was a draper and a gentleman and had a massive house built that stretched from the banks of the river right up to the start of the Wyle Cop. As he was a draper it would be fair to say that he was obviously extremely rich and he was in fact the very first Mayor of Shrewsbury but that still does not answer the question as to why so many orbs are on that site, unless ...

Remember the Abbots House in Butcher Row? That had a grey mist whizzing around inside it because of all the animals that were slaughtered on the spot. As Mr Jones was a draper he would have had to kill quite a few sheep for their wool and he would have had enough space do that in his back yard so these orbs could be the energy from the sheep! Eureeka!

Or could it have been from the Black Death when over 1,700 people succumbed to this dreadful disease and were buried in or under three small chapels, one of which was, 'By the banks of the Severn close to the Stone, (English), Bridge'. Oh well, back to the drawing board.

FIFTEEN

ROWLEY'S MANSION

In one of the buildings in Shrewsbury there are sightings of ghosts that seem to ignore each other despite appearing in the same room. This building is an old Tudor house known locally as Rowley's Mansion.

Towards the end of the 1590s William Rowley had started business as a draper, buying and selling wool and cloth. He was also a brewer and a carrier and had this fine house built for him. Later, around 1615, his son built the first brick-constructed house in Shrewsbury to house the brewing part of the business.

Rowley's Mansion is at the present time of writing a museum housing the town's artefacts and a major art centre for visiting artists. On the top floor they have a complete Tudor bedroom which holds a travelling four-poster bed that was once owned by the Corbet family (Remember them? They didn't have a house to live in thanks to Mr Holmyard). The ghost of lady Jane Corbet who died during childbirth is said to be seen on the bed at various times.

Although the bed is much travelled, having been included in displays of fine Tudor artefacts at various country houses around Britain, Lady Jane's ghost has been seen wherever the bed comes to rest. Also in the same room at Rowley's Mansion can be seen the ghost of a young man – could he be the young Lord Corbet keeping an eye on his wife but if so he doesn't speak to her, or could it be another memory ghost of another long past owner of the house? Maybe one of the Rowleys themselves.

In the Rowley's Tudor room hangs a painting of Old Parr. Born just outside Shrewsbury, Thomas Parr is reputed to have been 153 years old when he died. Not only was he one of the oldest men to have lived but it is said that he married for the first time at the age of eighty and fathered two children, and then married again when he was 120 and had another child!

The King wanted to see this old man but the journey to London was to much for him and he sadly passed away, but he is buried in Westminster Abbey. There is no known ghost of Thomas Parr but I reckon he would be to shattered to walk anyhow and just wanted a long rest!

Until the early part of the 1900s most of this house was hidden by other buildings but when they were demolished in the 1960s this was the result. Lady Corbet's bed is on the top floor through the left-hand window.

SIXTEEN

THE PARADE SHOPPING CENTRE

Another much haunted building is the Parade Shopping Centre. The Parade is in fact the old Royal Shrewsbury Infirmary which was built in the early 1700s. In the basement outside what used to be the hospital dispensary stands the ghost of Fred. When the hospital was built it included a soup kitchen that was put there to give the local parish poor a hot meal during the winter months. Fred is dressed wearing brown knee breeches and a green top and waits for someone to hand him his soup. He eventually gets fed up of waiting and fades away.

I worked at the hospital for seven years and my office was directly opposite where Fred used to appear and he made very frequent visits, sometimes up to eight or nine in a week, and so regular was he that all the staff would greet him as they passed. It used to give me great enjoyment when escorting a new member of staff to watch their faces as Fred faded away, and the staff member also disappeared for a while!

At the opposite end of the basement were the kitchens and the ghost of one of the Victorian matrons is still seen floating into the kitchen in the hope of getting a cup of tea from the cook after doing her daily morning ward rounds. The kitchen is now a coffee shop and many of its customers have reported feeling a presence walking past them as they enjoy a cuppa. What would happen if she asked for a piece of Victoria sponge? We might never know.

Another ghost that walks the old wards is the grey lady. We are not certain who this lady is but it is quite alarming that each and every time this lady was seen standing at the foot of a patient's bed then by morning that patient had passed away! It was obvious that for a long time the grey lady was regarded as a female version of the grim reaper but as time has gone on we now regard her more as the spirit of an old nurse who somehow knew that these patients were not going to survive and so came to 'look after' them. Interestingly, after some of her visitations it has been known for staff to actually move the patient to another ward but on each occasion the result was the same.

During the Second World War a Polish lady had collapsed in town and had been brought into the hospital and put on one of the wards. The doctor had asked a nurse to put an oxygen mask on the lady but she fought and fought and it was only when they managed to find an interpreter that the lady described seeing a Victorian nurse standing behind the doctor. Was this the matron on her rounds or another nurse? It wasn't the grey lady because the Polish visitor survived.

The imposing entrance to the RSI but it was only for use by surgeons and the like; we lesser mortals had to use the side entrance to the left!

Fred would appear outside the dispensary by the fire hose, waiting for his bowl of soup which never came!

The matron would appear at the far end by the stairs.

The top three floors of the old Royal Salop Infirmary are now private flats but some of the residents say that they can still hear moans and groans on quiet nights. Next door to the RSI is the old nursing home and that has also been converted to flats. One lady resident has a regular gentleman visitor who appears carrying a clip board. I don't think it's Eamon Andrews but where this lady's flat is situated used to be the chief engineer's office, and he always walked around with a clip board. Another memory ghost? I think so.

SEVENTEEN

DOGPOLE

Another of the old original roads that leads out of Shrewsbury's town centre and joins the Wyle Cop is Dogpole. It is so named because there used to be a stream that ran from the top of Butcher Row and then passed through a hole in the town wall before wending its way down behind the shops on the Cop and into the river.

Partway down Dogpole is an old house. It is possibly one of the oldest houses in Shrewsbury and is simply called The Old House. It contains two ghosts; one of them is a gentleman who is seen walking across the main entrance hall and then walking down a flight of steps into what used to be a kitchen. After he has disappeared down the stairs the sound of chopping wood is heard and after a while the smell of freshly cooked bacon wafts up the stairs. This, I think, is one of the ghosts returning to apologise for something he has done in the past.

When Mary, Queen of Scots was arrested it was the Earl of Shrewsbury who supplied part of the escort who took her to her execution and, interestingly, at each castle or house that Mary stopped at on her final journey they all experience the same ghost, a man who walks into the old kitchens and the chopping of wood is heard and bacon is on the menu that day.

The other ghost that appears is a lady who stands looking out of a window at the passing traffic before she turns and walks through a wooden panel in the wall next to the chimney. Recently, the owners have discovered a small passage behind the chimney that leads to a very small private chapel. Who this lady is we don't know but there is some thoughts that Mary herself stayed in the house. As she was a Catholic supporter she may have needed somewhere private where she could say her prayers so maybe, just maybe, we might have a royal visitor.

Another strange sighting that has come to light in recent months is that of a large Labrador-type dog that sits at the top of the steps. No one knows, as yet, who owns the dog but photographs of it are beginning to come to light.

On the opposite side of the road of The Old House is a shop that stands on the site of the original Eye, Ear, Nose and Throat Hospital. The owner of the shop has reported many times that if she is working in the back of the shop when a customer comes in, they are often attended to first by a young girl of about eight years old. Once the shop owner walks in, then the young lass turns and walks upstairs and out of sight, leaving a lot of the customers to comment on how polite the little girl is!

The main door is set back so cannot be seen in this photo but the lady, Mary? Is seen in the front bay window

Site of the old Eye, Ear, Nose and Throat Hospital. The hospital's morgue was below the shop front.

EIGHTEEN

AROUND OLD ST CHAD'S

One of the saddest sites where a ghost, or ghosts, appear is in the bookshop on the corner of Princess Street and College Hill, opposite the Old St Chad's church. Often known as Bert Dans newspaper shop, which it was a long time ago, it is the site of a particularly tragic occurrence.

In the early 1800s a fire broke out in the area and all the houses were destroyed. In this particular house the ghosts of three children are seen huddled together on the top landing as if they are waiting for someone to come and rescue them. On the stairwell below them is another ghost, that of the children's nanny who attempted, but failed, to rescue them.

Also, on the first flight of stairs, as people are walking up to the next floor they suddenly stop and clutch their chests and explain that they feel like someone has just stabbed them. I don't think that this particular spirit has any connection with the fire but is another spirit from a different time, possibly a residue from a long past fight or other misdemeanour.

Faces can sometimes be seen looking out of the top window.

NINETEEN

OUT IN THE COUNTRYSIDE PART 2

Let's pop out into the countryside to get a bit more fresh air, and other things. During Saxon times, Shropshire's answer to Robin Hood was Wild Edric. Edric and his wife, together with his fellow men, are said to haunt the Stiperstones. Legend has it that Edric was fooled by the Normans and imprisoned in the mines but because he was a true believer in this merry England, his ghost, and that of his men, are allowed out only when the country is in danger and when that happens it is said that Edric and his men will gallop off in the direction that the enemy will come from. Sightings of Edric were reported at the beginning of the Crimean War, and the Napoleonic Wars, and at the beginnings of the two world wars. Edric's wife, Godda, is said to carry a large jewel-encrusted sword into battle, but is it for her or for Edric?

In Chetwynd, near Newport, there is the ghost of a lady who died in childbirth over 200 years ago. Her ghost walks from the church towards a large Elizabethan mansion where she once lived. Locals say that if a tree in the grounds of the mansion begins to shake even when there is no wind then she is combing her child's hair.

Condover Hall, just to the south of Shrewsbury, was until recently the centre for the Royal National Institute for the Blind but some 300 years ago a dreadful murder was committed. The owner of the hall, Lord Knyvett, was murdered by his son during a heated argument. After the sheriff had been called to view the stabbed body, the son blamed the murder on the butler who was promptly arrested and convicted of the crime. As the butler was led to the gallows he put a curse on the hall and the owners, and vowed that no one who was related to the family would ever prosper. And it seems that the curse worked until the 1980s.

After Lord Knyvett had been stabbed he staggered down some steps and where he fell on the steps he left an imprint in blood of his hand which defied all attempts to remove it until the whole step was cut away and replaced. Very definitely what the butler saw!

In Atcham, a small village on the A5 heading eastwards, is the Mytton Hotel. Originally called the Mytton and Mermaid, it gets its name from a local landowner, Jack, or Mad Jack, Mytton.

Jack was a bit of a character and there are many stories about him. One such is that he crawled in his nightshirt one bleak winter's day to go duck shooting and to cure his coldness, promptly set fire to his shirt!

Jack died in a prison and on his birthday 30 September, his ghost is said to walk through the hotel even though for many years the local priest would exorcise the building the day before.

Mad Jack Mytton's Hotel in Atcham. To the rear is St Etas, the parish church. Both buildings sit on the banks of the Severn.

Just beyond Atcham is the site of the Roman city of *Viriconium*, now known as Wroxeter. *Viriconium* dates from the first century and is reputed to be the fifth largest Roman city in England, being about 170 acres in size. Even Emperor Hadrian visited it, but didn't build his wall. Only part of the city is still on view with a lot of the other foundations hidden under the farm land now surrounding it, but on its westerly edge is the Wroxeter vineyards. The vineyard produces around 40,000 bottles of wine a year and the owners have won numerous awards at wine gatherings all over Europe. Customers to the vineyard can take a guided walk around the site but many have felt that there is an extra person on the tour. Indeed, you have the feeling that maybe a legionnaire is escorting you as he would have done all those hundreds of years ago.

At Cardington is an Elizabethan house that has the ghost of a man who walks the upper floors. The house was built by a local judge and at the assizes he was trying a local builder. After he had sentenced him to the gallows he approached the man in his cell and made a bargain with him. If he could design a chimney for his new house then he would be spared.

Naturally the builder set to and came up with some wonderful designs which the judge loved so much that he had them built on his house, and then executed the poor man! The builder's ghost is still looking for the judge, and there is a lady who wanders the hall as well – could she be someone else from a different time, or could she be the builder's wife?

Hopton Castle in the south of the county is said to be haunted by soldiers from the Civil War. Around forty men who were supporters of the parliament were surrounded by royalists

The vines stand just like Roman soldiers at Wroxeter vineyards. But beware as you walk around as you could be escorted by a Hadrian or a Brutus.

and held to siege for nearly three weeks. At the end of that time, rather than be taken every man committed suicide and it is their ghosts that still walk the ruins after dark.

Myddle Castle, to the north-west of Shrewsbury, is just a tower now but it is said that the ghost of Humphrey Kynaston, a local bandit who once owned the castle before he fell into hard times and had to take to the road, still rides around the grounds.

Between Myddle and Harmer Hill runs the Lower Road, and during the Second World War a four-engined aircraft on 'circles and bumps' from Sleap airfield crashed into the soft sandstone of the hill, leaving a perfect imprint of the engines. Sadly the hill has now been quarried out but the aircraft can still be heard flying on its final mission.

Wem, nine miles north of Shrewsbury, had a great fire about 400 years ago when most of the centre of the town was destroyed. Among the burned down buildings was the town hall and in the conflagration a young lady called Jane Churms, who people think actually started the fire, was killed. In the mid-1980s Wem had a second fire at the rebuilt town hall and a local photographer filming the blaze snapped a photograph that showed Jane standing on the stairs again. Did she start this second fire like it was thought she had the first? Who knows.

So, that's a few more visitors to Shropshire that have been around for a few centuries – let's go back to Shrewsbury for a nice cup of tea.

TWENTY

MILK STREET

One of the timber-framed buildings in Milk Street houses the Poppy's Tudor Tearooms.

Milk Street, standing at the top of the Wyle Cop opposite Fish Street, was so named because milk and cheese were sold there during the old market times. And the house in question probably started life as a shop before changing to become a public house. Pub names changed almost as many times as the landlord changed barrels but by 1895 the name had become 'The Sun' and that is how it stayed until it became a gunsmiths in 1910 before changing to its present form in the 1970s. Poppy's has six extra customers that appear in various rooms that Chris has found.

A family group dating from the 1700s are in the house with the two children, one named Emily and the other called Jack seen on the stairs. Jack is very impish and will open and close the front door every now and again. Their mother can be found in the upper restaurant room and the father is in a front room, now a staff room, standing in front of the window smoking a pipe.

At the rear of Poppy's is a small courtyard which is now a seating area and Chris has found a coachman who wears a tall hat and a long coat. Chris gets the feeling that his name could be Dhomas – not Thomas but Dhomas. He looks up to the top floor where a ghost of a maid can be found. Both these last two ghosts date back to 1875 but are they connected? Chris senses that they seem to know each other well – could they be husband and wife, lovers or just friends? Maybe we shall never know.

Standing on the corner of Milk Stret and High Street stands The Wheatsheaf public house. The Wheatsheaf has been here for some time but is another of the pubs that has changed its name over the time but it retains its customers, including the spirit ones. Standing behind the bar is the ghost of a small child who delights in moving glasses, especially full ones, around the room and there is also a 'memory ghost' of a coachman who although not a very regular visitor, still attends.

In the Square stands the music hall, at the time of writing it is the main theatre in Shrewsbury but will soon become one of the town's largest museums when our new theatre is built on the banks of the Severn. An old friend of mine who used to be the manager and tourism officer at the music hall up to the mid-1980s tells the story of a ghost that haunts the upper changing rooms. Sadly the sightings of this ghost are few and far between but we are told that as the staff

Above: *Frontage of Poppy's. The father, or traces of his tobacco, is in the top room to the left.*

Left: *Jack and Emily can often be seen on these stairs. Jack thinks it is fun to open the front door every now and again, naughty Jack!*

Opposite above: *View from the maid's room of Poppy's, looking out for Dhomas.*

Opposite below: *Behind the topmost windows of the music hall are dressing rooms and a ghost scared of the dark. What is she, scared of spirits or something?*

The Admiral Benbow stands waiting for its coachman to return.

do the nightly rounds of locking up, they start at the top of the building and work down but as they finish and are walking across the square, on looking back they see that the lights are on in the top rooms, after they have turned them off.

Behind the music hall on Swan Hill stands the Admiral Benbow pub. Named after the famous admiral who was a distant relative of our Captain John Benbow of Civil War fame, the pub was originally called the Talbot Tap as it was connected to the now long-gone Talbot Coaching Hotel that used to stand next to the music hall in the Square.

The first record of the name Admiral Benbow appeared in 1861 and it was because our admiral was born in Shrewsbury and ran away to sea to become one of our greatest seafarers and defeated the French in the West Indies. Sadly he died of his wounds and is buried in Jamaica.

The figure of a man stands at the rear of the pub dressed in a long black cloak and, although I can hear you say 'Not another coachman', you must remember that the centre of Shrewsbury was highly populated in ale houses and the beer was much stronger way back then so it's no wonder that a lot of deaths occurred after fights over money, women or even just a bet that went the wrong way.

So our man stands at the back of the pub and is quite a cheerful character which is one thing about most of the ghosts in Shrewsbury.

We don't have a lot of chilling ghosts, most of them are just like the townsfolk of Shrewsbury, quiet, peaceful and happy. They just get on with what they are doing and of course our spirit people have walked these roads and streets long before us so why not let them keep enjoying the atmosphere?

If required, Martin can lead you on a ghost tour of Shrewsbury.
To contact him telephone: 07718951902

Other local titles published by The History Press

Haunted Birmingham
ARTHUR SMITH AND RACHEL BANNISTER

From creepy happenings in the city centre to stories of phantoms in the theatres, pubs and hospitals, this book contains a chilling range of ghostly tales. Drawing on historical and contemporary sources the authors tell of a landlady who haunts her old pub, two dead workmen who came back to haunt the town hall and an ex-mayor who still watches over the city. Scary stuff!

978 07524 4017 0

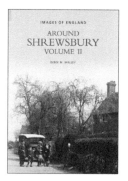

Around Shrewsbury Volume 2
DEREK M. WALLEY

All aspects of everyday life are recorded here, from shops and businesses, churches and schools, to images of work and leisure, day trips and days off. The landscapes and landmarks of the town and its surrounding areas are captured in this valuable historical record of life in Shrewsbury as it used to be.

978 07524 3371 4

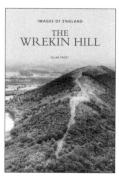

The Wrekin Hill
ALLAN FROST

The Wrekin Hill was, and still is, a playground for people, many of whom still visit its famous Halfway House for refreshment after squeezing through the Needle's Eye and remember the luncheons, dinners, dances and hospitality at the Forest Glen Pavilions ... and the age-old toast to 'All friends round The Wrekin'. This book not only gives a fascinating insight into the unique history of a hill whose name has spread throughout the world but also includes an abundance of illustrations.

978 07524 4256 3

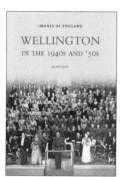

Wellington in the 1940s and '50s
ALLAN FROST

This collection of archive photographs documents life in the historic Shropshire market town of Wellington during and after the Second World War. Entertaining and informative, this book reveals how the people of Wellington coped with severe rationing and how they found enjoyment in a wide range of activities. *Wellington in the 1940s and '50s* is an important pictorial history which will delight all who have lived or worked here.

978 07524 3767 5

If you are interested in purchasing other books published by The History Press, or in case you have difficulty finding any of our books in your local bookshop, you can also place orders directly through our website
www.thehistorypress.co.uk

This book is dedicated to my wife, Sue.

First published in 2007 by Tempus Publishing

Reprinted in 2010 by
The History Press
The Mill, Brimscombe Port,
Stroud, Gloucestershire, GL5 2QG
www.thehistorypress.co.uk

Reprinted 2011, 2012

British Library Cataloguing in Publication Data.
A catalogue record for this book is available from the British Library.

ISBN 978 0 7524 4303 4

Typesetting and origination by
Tempus Publishing
Printed and bound in England.